745.592 Fel
elix, Rebecca,
ool action figures & dolls :
rafting creative toys & amazing games
28.50

3   4028   09610   7421
HARRIS COUNTY PUBLIC LIBRARY

W9-DGU-258

COOL
ACTION FIGURES & DOLLS
CRAFTING CREATIVE TOYS & AMAZING GAMES

REBECCA
FELIX

Checkerboard
Library

An Imprint of Abdo Publishing
abdopublishing.com

ABDOPUBLISHING.COM

Published by Abdo Publishing, a division of ABDO, PO Box 398166, Minneapolis, Minnesota 55439. Copyright © 2016 by Abdo Consulting Group, Inc. International copyrights reserved in all countries. No part of this book may be reproduced in any form without written permission from the publisher. Checkerboard Library™ is a trademark and logo of Abdo Publishing.

Printed in the United States of America, North Mankato, Minnesota

102015
012016

THIS BOOK CONTAINS
RECYCLED MATERIALS

Content Developer: Nancy Tuminelly
Design and Production: Mighty Media, Inc.
Editor: Liz Salzmann
Photo Credits: AP Images, Ivan_Sabo/Shutterstock, Mighty Media, Inc., PAISAN HOMHUAN/ Shutterstock, Pavel L Photo and Video/Shutterstock, Radu Bercan/Shutterstock, Shutterstock

The following manufacturers/names appearing in this book are trademarks:
Barbie®, Coke®, Craft Smart®

Library of Congress Cataloging-in-Publication Data
Felix, Rebecca, 1984- author.
  Cool action figures & dolls : crafting creative toys & amazing games / by Rebecca Felix.
      pages cm. -- (Cool toys & games)
  Includes index.
  ISBN 978-1-68078-045-1
1. Toy making--Juvenile literature. 2. Dollmaking--Juvenile literature. I. Title. II. Title: Cool action figures and dolls.
  TT174.F45 2016
  745.592--dc23
                    2015033098

CONTENTS

DOLLS AND ACTION FIGURES

Dolls are thought to be the world's oldest toys. The world's oldest doll was dug up on an Italian island. It was 4,000 years old!

ITALY

ISLAND WHERE THE OLDEST DOLL WAS FOUND

MEDITERRANEAN SEA

4

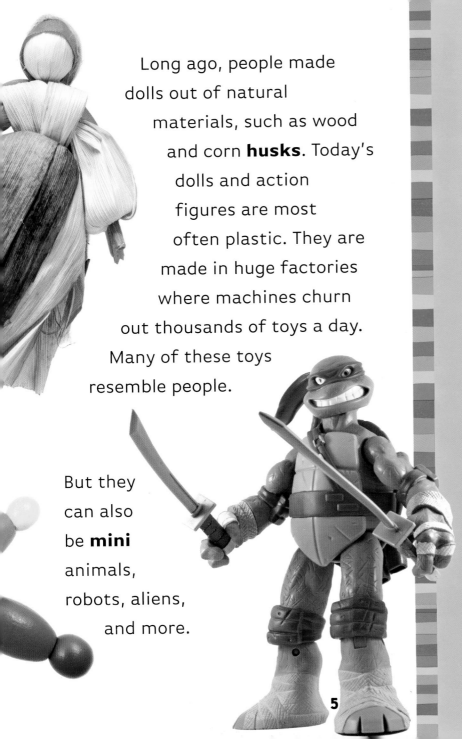

Long ago, people made dolls out of natural materials, such as wood and corn **husks**. Today's dolls and action figures are most often plastic. They are made in huge factories where machines churn out thousands of toys a day. Many of these toys resemble people.

But they can also be **mini** animals, robots, aliens, and more.

THE FIRST ACTION FIGURES

In the 1960s, girls loved Barbie dolls. Another toy company thought boys would like a male doll just as much. The company created a US soldier toy called G. I. Joe.

G. I. Joes were the first action figures. This name was more appealing to boys than *dolls*.

Soon, G. I. Joes were not only soldiers. They were astronauts, superheroes, and more. Today, there are more than 500 G. I. Joe characters!

5

MAKING MINI BODIES, HEADS, AND MORE

Think of dolls and action figures you have played with. Some might be simple, with heads and bodies made of one piece. Others might have many little parts.

Action figures can have different types of hair, clothing, and **accessories**. Some even come with **mini** pets! Many toy makers around the world work each day making these parts.

HIDDEN TREASURE

Matryoshkas are Russian nesting dolls. They are made of wood. Matryoshkas take years to make! The wood has to dry for two years before it can be carved.

Toy makers include hair, clothing, and makeup designers. Some people operate special machines that mold plastic into limbs, bodies, and **accessories**.

Other workers sew hair onto dolls and dress action figures in costumes. Once the toys are assembled, they are packaged and shipped.

DOLLS OF ALL SIZES

Dolls come in all sizes. One in England is smaller than a dime. The world's largest rag doll is taller than a giraffe!

20 FEET (6 M)

11/16 INCH (18 MM)

BECOME A
TOY MAKER

THINK LIKE A TOY MAKER

Present-day dolls and action figures are pretty amazing. They come in many shapes, sizes, and colors. There are baby dolls, robots, aliens, and more!

Some dolls have hair that changes colors. Action figures can swim, or even fly! Even the simplest dolls can go on adventures. All they need is your imagination!

8

As you work on the projects in this book, think like a toy maker. Read the steps and look at the photos. Get inspired. Then get creative!

HAVE FUN!

Having fun is a big part of toy making. Maybe you want your doll to wear a costume, have a pet, or carry an umbrella. Go for it! Search at home or in craft stores for fun things to add to your creations. The action figures and dolls you create are meant to be **unique**! Use your imagination as you prepare for the projects in this book. Then have fun making some toys!

MATERIALS

acrylic paint

adhesive hook & loop tape

aluminum foil

cardboard

chenille stems

craft foam

craft sticks

empty containers

feathers

found objects

hot glue gun & glue sticks

mini springs

old magazines
and calendars

old suitcase

paintbrush

parchment
paper

polymer clay

pom-poms

string

toothpicks

twigs

SAFETY SYMBOLS

Some projects in this book use sharp objects or require eye protection. This means these projects need adult help. You may see one or more safety symbols at the beginning of a project. Here is what they mean:

 HOT

 GOGGLES

TWIG THINGS

CREATE COOL CREATURES, ALIENS, OR DOLLS OUT OF TWIGS!

PREP THE TWIGS

1 Gather small branches and twigs from outside.

2 Decide how large you want your Twig Thing to be. Put on the safety goggles. Break the twigs into different sizes for the body, arms, and legs.

3 Peel loose bark from the twigs. Then use sandpaper to smooth the broken ends and edges.

(continued on next page)

MATERIALS

twigs of various sizes
safety goggles
sandpaper
hot glue gun & glue sticks
chenille stems
rubber bands

embroidery thread
pencil
googly eyes
pom-poms
sequins

BUILD THE BODY

1 Time to connect the twigs to build a body! There are several ways to do this.

2 Connect twigs with hot glue. Be sure to let the glue dry.

3 Wrap a chenille stem around the twigs to hold them together.

4 You can also use rubber bands or embroidery thread to connect twigs.

DECORATE!

1 Wrap your Twig Thing with chenille stems.

2 Make hands, feet, and hair from chenille stems too. Wrap the stems around a pencil to make curly hair or antennas.

3 Attach googly eyes with hot glue. You can also add pom-poms, sequins, or other decorations.

4 Make your Twig Thing as wild as you like. Then make more Twig Things!

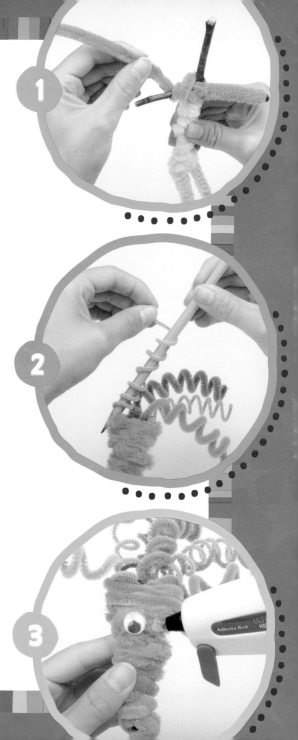

BARBIE ADVENTURE CASE

BUILD A PORTABLE CASE FULL OF FUN ACTIVITIES AND DESTINATIONS!

PREP THE SUITCASE

1 Open the suitcase. Cut off any belts or straps.

2 Cut several strips of the scratchy side of the hook and loop tape. Stick them vertically inside the bottom of the suitcase.

3 Cut more strips of the scratchy side of the hook and loop tape. Lay the lid on a flat surface and stick the pieces **horizontally** inside the suitcase lid.

(continued on next page)

MATERIALS

old suitcase
scissors
adhesive hook & loop tape
old magazines and calendars
glue stick
cardboard

felt
craft foam
stapler & staples
craft sticks
rocks
pinecones
small animal figurines
Barbie accessories

17

CREATE ADVENTURE BACKGROUNDS

1 Cut **landscape** and **landmark** photos out of old magazines or calendars. Look for pictures of animals too. You can also search for photos online and print them.

2 Cut out the animals. Glue them to larger landscape images to create adventure scene **collages**.

3 Use the glue stick to attach your scenes to cardboard. Trim extra cardboard from the sides.

4 Cut several strips of the soft side of the hook and loop tape. Stick them **horizontally** to the back of the cardboard.

5 Press a scene in the bottom of the suitcase. Set the suitcase with the lid flat on a table or the floor.

ACCESSORIES AND ADVENTURES!

1 Cut pieces of felt to extend your scenes. Make them as big as the inside of the lid. Try blue for water, green for grass, or brown for sand. Press the felt inside the suitcase lid.

2 Create **accessories**. Make a boat out of craft foam and oars out of the craft sticks. Add rocks, pinecones, and animals to the scene. Get creative!

3 Send your Barbie on an adventure! Then change the scene whenever you like. Store the accessories inside the suitcase when you're not using them.

WORLD'S MOST FAMOUS DOLL

Barbie has been called "the most famous doll in history." The company that makes them says three Barbies are sold every second around the world!

20

Ruth Handler created the Barbie doll in the 1950s. At the time, many US children played with baby dolls. While vacationing in Europe, Handler noticed kids there had dolls that resembled adults. Her idea for Barbie was born.

Handler got to work planning and designing. She named the doll after her daughter, Barbara. The Barbie doll was first sold in 1959. It was soon wildly successful. Today, Barbies are sold in 150 countries!

BARBIE BUSINESS

More than 100 people work together to create each new Barbie **prototype**. It is a lot of work! Toy makers spend months drawing, designing, and creating before the new Barbie is ready to be **mass-produced**.

FOUND-OBJECT ACTION FIGURE

CREATE A ONE-OF-A-KIND ACTION FIGURE FROM ALL KINDS OF THINGS!

1 Gather some small objects. Almost anything can work! Look in your recycling and outside too.

2 Decide which object will be the body. Then decorate it. You could wrap it in rubber bands or aluminum foil. You could also paint it or glue things to it.

3 Use hot glue to attach limbs and a head. Or look for other ways to attach things. Maybe you could stick limbs through the body or attach them with rubber bands.

4 Glue on objects to make a face. Then add any cool features you like. Have fun and be creative!

MATERIALS

hot glue gun & glue sticks
scissors
OPTIONAL:
crayons
markers

acrylic paint
paintbrush
FOUND OBJECTS, SUCH AS:
aluminum foil
beads
buttons

craft foam
empty containers
golf tees
keys
magnets
old jewelry

paper clips
pencils
rubber bands
scrap paper
soda bottles and cans
string

toilet paper tubes
wire

SPRINGY SPRITES

SCULPT SUPERCOOL CLAY ACTION FIGURES THAT HAVE BOBBLING HEADS, ARMS, AND LEGS!

MATERIALS

aluminum foil
polymer clay
mini springs
dinner knife
toothpicks
parchment
 paper
baking sheet
oven mitts
hot glue gun &
 glue sticks

OPTIONAL

beads
chenille stems
feathers
felt
string

1 Roll aluminum foil into a small ball or rectangle. Cover it with a thin layer of clay. This will be the action figure's body. The foil makes the body lighter than if it were solid clay.

2 Roll, pinch, and mold clay into arms and legs.

3 Make a small ball of foil for the head. Cover it with clay.

(continued on next page)

TRY THIS!

Make colorful body parts! Blend two or more colors of clay together.

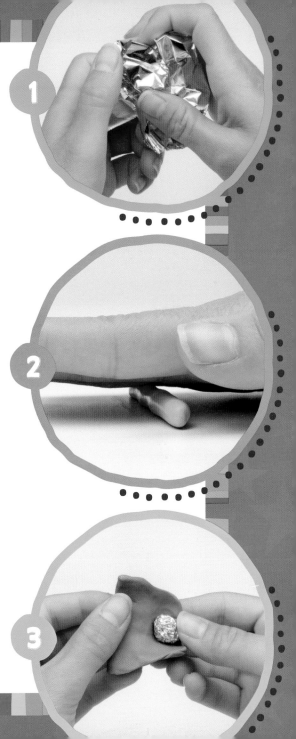

4 Gently twist the end of a spring into the head. Attach springs to the limbs the same way.

5 Twist the other end of each spring into the body to attach the head and limbs.

6 Use a dinner knife and toothpick to cut and form small features out of clay.

7 Press the features onto the figure.

TRY THIS!

*Create **accessories** out of clay! Your action figure's limbs move. So you can make it kick a clay ball, carry a clay purse, walk a clay animal, or play a clay instrument!*

8 Place a piece of parchment paper on the baking sheet. Place the clay figure on the paper.

9 Preheat the oven to 275 degrees Fahrenheit (135ºC). Put the baking sheet in the oven. Bake for 15 minutes. Carefully check whether the clay has hardened. If it is still soft, bake for another 15 minutes.

10 Take the baking sheet out of the oven. Let the figure cool. Use hot glue to add hair or other fun features.

11 Make more springy action figures. Then think of fun adventures for them to go on!

SECRET-CONTAINER CREATURE

STORE ALL KINDS OF STUFF INSIDE AN ACTION FIGURE THAT IS A SECRET CONTAINER!